NEW IDEAS WITH PARCHMENT CRAFT

more possibilities with parchment paper

*Pergamano** is the tradename under which the designs and materials for the parchment craft is put on the market.

Did you know there is a parchment craft magazine which tells you all about this wonderful hobby? Pergamano World is a bi-monthly magazine, issued by Marjo-Arte in the Netherlands and is exclusively dedicated to the creative craft with parchment paper, and it is meant for people the world over.

Pergamano World provides you with:
- patterns with working instructions
- full colour pictures of ready-made articles
- lessons in techniques by Martha Ospina
- tips and hints for your practise
- etc.

Pergamano World contains among other things:
- pen pal page
- reports from correspondents from all around the world

If you would like to know more about Pergamano World, please write to:
Marjo-Arte B.V.
P.O. Box 2288
1180 EG Amstelveen
The Netherlands

4th Edition, 1995

First published by La Rivière & Voorhoeve, Baarn The Netherlands in 1990
Photography: Ton Kruithof, Kampen
Typesetting: Stand By, Nieuwegein
Printing: Van der Weij B.V. Grafische Bedrijven, Hilversum The Netherlands

ISBN 90 384 0690 8
NUGI 440

MARTHA OSPINA

NEW IDEAS WITH PARCHMENT CRAFT

more possibilities with parchment paper

CONTENTS

INTRODUCTION

Pergamano-2 is the sequel to Martha Ospina's first book PERGAMANO – Cards made from parchment paper (ISBN 90 384 0343 7 – La Rivière & Voorhoeve). The parchment paper used in the making of parchment craft pieces has special properties which makes it possible for the easy tracing of patterns, embossing, painting, dorsing (colouring the back of the paper) and the hallmark of the work, paper lace work. This creative hobby has its roots in Spanish convents at the time of Christopher Colombus and nuns then used real parchment. With the discovery of South America by Colombus the Spanish church introduced not only religion but also this ecclesiastical craft into Colombia and other South American countries. The craft has been practiced through the centuries and also expanded so that it now encompasses not only the original embossing and lace work but also tracing, painting etc. Martha Ospina introduced this craft from her native Colombia into Europe where it has become the rage.

Properties of parchment paper

Spanish nuns

Parchment craft pieces are not only original, but works of art. You can make greetings cards to cover all occasions i. e. birthdays, first communions, births etc. You can also make decorative envelopes in which to put gifts of money or vouchers, bookmarks, menu cards, brooches and pictures for the wall. The many techniques used in parchment craft give you a wide choice of designs which means that cards can be personalised (especially if you are good at calligraphy) for special occasions. Or, if you cannot bear to part with them, keep them in an album to show to friends. Many of the lace edged cards are reminiscent of early Victorian cards and collectors of such cards are always delighted with pachment work and will avidly pour over your album of work.

The beauty of the craft and its varied techniques means that you can produce a 'different' card from the simplest techniques. Beginners find to their delight that they have made a workpiece to be proud of using only the tracing and embossing techniques.

Greetings cards

Brooches
Pictures

Easy

With the techniques varying from simple to the more skilled it means that everyone can enjoy this craft. If you are of an artistic bent it also means that you can produce your own exclusive disigns based on the many techniques.
This book continues on from the first book and the basic techniques covered in it are not contained in this book which deals with more advanced techniques.

Basis techniques are not repeated

The special materials required for this craft are now in the art and hobby shops in several countries. If you cannot find them, write to Pergamano World Service (P.W.S.), P.O. BOX 2288 Amstelveen, The Netherlands.

1. ADVANCING YOUR BASIC TECHNIQUES

Tracing
Painting
Embossing
Perforating
Cutting

As mentioned in the introduction this book does not cover the basic techniques and assumes that you are well versed in tracing, painting with TINTA (inks), PINTURA (paints), colouring with DORSO pastels and those of embossing, perforating and cutting. Here we are going to look at making pieces that have depth.
Previously we were making flat pieces such as bookmarks and cards although some patterns have contained pricked out work that was then stuck onto the finished piece or a piece of the card was perforated out. Another way to achieve a 3-D effect is to use PERGAKIT, a type of glue that holds on parchment paper.

3-D Method

Pattern 8 in the chapter 5.1 'Patterns' is a 3-Dimensional piece and the method of doing this is as follows: Make the card as per the instructions given remembering to paint the card in the given colours as well as the 3-D pieces which are: the flame, the candle wax, flowers and the 4 baubles. Emboss these pieces lightly so as to give them form then perforate or cut them out of the spare piece of paper that they were traced onto and place them on the card in their correct positions. Using the PERGAKIT and a wooden cocktail stick, squeeze about

Pergakit

3mm of PERGAKIT out and remove from the tube with the cocktail stick, lift the piece to be stuck and place the dot of PERGAKIT in the middle of the correct placing and then put the 3-D piece on top and press lightly into place. The PERGAKIT will take about 3 hours to dry and will remain pliable even when dry. When making cards with larger 3-D pieces you may well require more dots of silicone to secure the piece. Use this technique for making the 'Winter landscape' pattern in chapter 5.2.

Adheres well

Not too large
A piece of Pergakit

Cutting away waste parchment paper from card edges

This can be done in different ways:

a. With a sharp craft knife and a ruler.
b. Folding the parchment paper, making a sharp fold, and using strong cotton (available from needlework shops) to cut the paper as per the photograph. With this method you create a rough edge which looks good and goes with the character of the parchment paper.
c. Using a single needle tool to perforate round the edge of the card (i.e. on a wavy edge) and then gently pull away the waste paper.

Sharp craft knife
Strong cotton thread

Single needle tool

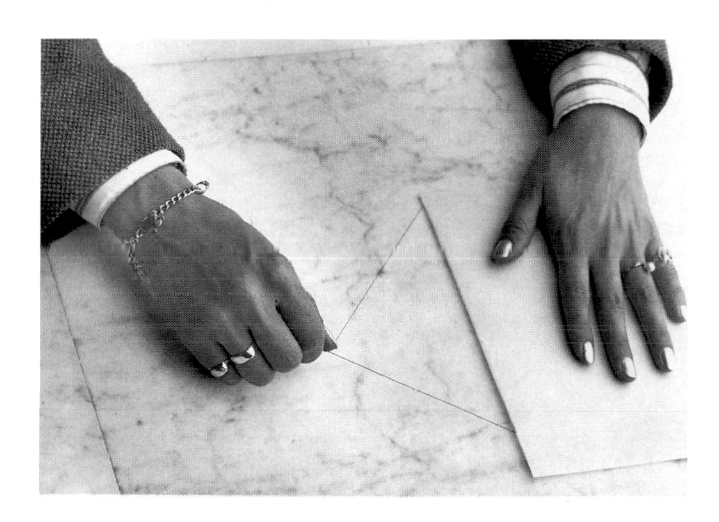

Pinking shears

d. After using method a. or b. you can then go over the edge with a pair of pinking shears.

e. On a card that has a lace border you can cut the paper between the crosses of the outer edge.

Sharp pointed scissors

f. Cut along the edge with a pair of ordinary scissors to create a wavy edge or use a special pair of 'wavy' scissors.

2. PERFORATION GRIDS

Making your own designs

Perforating and cutting technique

Probably the most well known hallmark of parchment cards is the perforated and cut lace work. The use of embossing in the perforation grid with such things as flowers, stars, etc. give the card an extra special touch.

Make your own perforation grid

You have probably only used the grids as shown in the patterns up till now but it is possible to make your own perforated designs. When you know the basic method of making these it is not difficult then to go on and make your own designs and variations.

Millimetre Paper
Sharp pointed pencil

All that is necessary to create your own lace work is:

- an A4 sheet of millimetre graph paper
- a pencil with a very sharp point
- a good eraser

As you already know the points in the grids are always 1 mm apart as per the 4 needle tool so by using 1 millimetre graph paper a dot in each square will give you the correct width.

Four hole combination

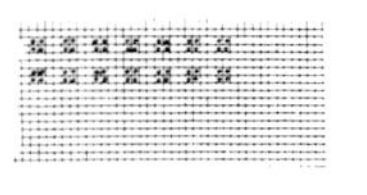

By putting the dots in groups of 4 we produce the dots in the 4 needle tool format. We call this a four hole combination which we can later cut out to make the well known cross-like hole.

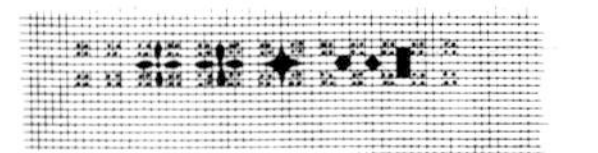

The simplist grid is created by leaving four squares between each four hole combination which can be used for drawing in a piece to be embossed. This could be a flower, star, dots, lines etc. In fact you can have any combination of these embossings in one grid if you want to.

When you are making your own designs do remember to make them so that they fit envelopes (see the chapter entitled 'helpful hints') and that your designs match up on the corners. Here are a number of examples of perforating patterns:

- Perforating to make slots: draw 3 x 4 hole combinations side by side so that they can be cut into slots or put them one on top of the other so that eventually a ribbon can be slotted through them (make sure that the slots are the right size for the ribbon).
- Perforating to make corner slots: make corner slots by drawing a line of 3 x 4 hole cobinations and to one side and under each other 2 x 4 hole combinations. Cut to a corner slot.
- See example B for making a corner in a grid pattern.
- See example C for a grid with room for a larger embossed pattern.
- See example D for a lace edge.

Dimension standard envelopes

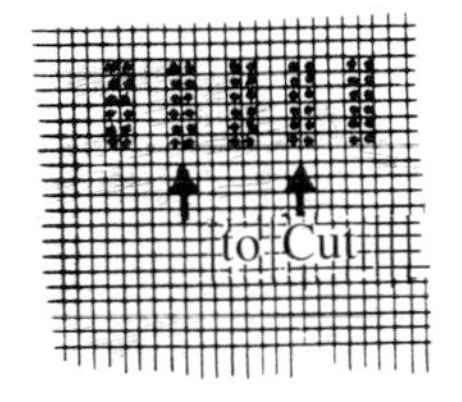

Corner slots

Corner

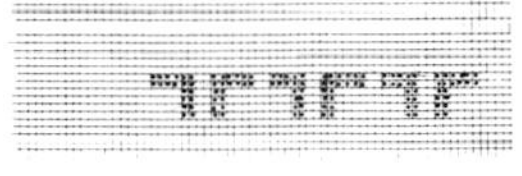

Space for embossed pattern

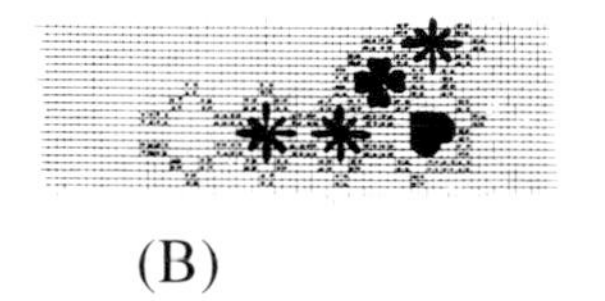

(B)

(C)

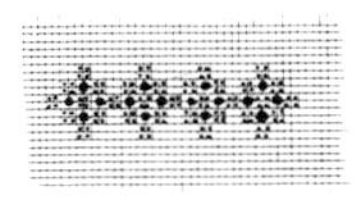

(D)

3. MAKING BROOCHES OR PENDANTS

Jewellery

Shape

Symmetrical pattern

Painting a miniature

My students have experimented with using parchment pieces in brooch or pendant blanks and have found that this jewellery looks superb.
You need an oval or round blank with a glass/plastic front with a diameter of approximately 5 cm. Once you have the blank of your choice remove the frame from the front and backing and place the frame onto millimetre graph paper. Using a pencil draw round the inner frame and mark the centre of the frame on the paper with a cross. This enables you to centre up a pattern so that it is symmetrical. Now you can make yourself a design to fit the blank using any or all the techniques of parchment craft.
If you choose to paint the design remember that the area of paint will be small like painting a miniature. You can lacquer the finished painting if you would like to give it extra shine.
Choose a background colour for your design which can be cut out of coloured paper or felt and use the backing piece of the blank as a cutting guide. If you have nothing in the colour of your choice you could always dorse a piece of parchment paper to the desired colour.
Put the brooch or pendant together. You can make jewellery this way to match any of your outfits.

4. HELPFUL HINTS

Plastic film

Barbecue igniter

I hope that the following hints will help you in your work:
- Patterns featuring perforation grids will last longer if you cover the pattern with self adhesive clear plastic.
- When dorsing a large piece of parchment paper you will find it easier to spread the dorso if you use a drop of lighter fuel or barbecue igniter on the cloth. If you use

more than a drop you can also clean the paper of any unwanted dorsing.

- If you want to write a greeting or message in a parchment craft card then use a paper insert and attach it to the card with either a ribbon or stitch through both thicknesses on the fold line. **Inserts**
- Always try out any message or greeting you wish to write on a spare piece of paper to see what it looks like and to ensure that you get it spaced correctly – if it is alright you can trace it onto the parchment paper. **Trying out**
- If you wish to highlight a piece of your work you can do so by using clear nail varnish.
- You have a blot of Tinta on your work! First suck it up by using the corner of a piece of kitchen paper, let it dry and then scrape away carefully using a razor blade or by using the parchment craft eraser. **Kitchen paper**
- If your white or gold Tinta has become too thick then you can thin it out by mixing in a little distilled water. **Distilled water**
- Having problems with gold or silver Tinta? Use a small stick and stir the tinta well making sure that the end of the stick reaches the bottom of the bottle. Bring the stick out and fill the pen by dropping the tinta onto the nib of the stick. **Stirring gold and silver ink**
- Perforations have torn – use a little transparent glue such as white wood glue, to repair the tear. The glue will dry transparent. **Transparent glue**
- Festive feeling – if you wish to bring a little glitter to your card then paint the area you want with a little clear nail varnish and scatter glitter over it. **Festive look**
- Albums to store your parchment craft cards in: use black pages that have the pull back self-adhesive plastic on. **Photo albums**
- It is always handy to bear in mind the sizes of standard envelopes that you can buy in the stationers when designing your cards. **Standard envelopes**

5. PATTERNS

5.1 GREETINGS CARDS

Birthday or New Year card

General GENERAL
For a New Year card the figure 1 appears on the calendar page. For a birthday card either the date or the age appears on the calendar page.
Choice of edges either 'a' or 'b' – mark the edge of the card with a white pencil then if you wish to use edge 'a' trace this with white ink so that you have a guide line to cut on. If you want just a straight edge or the pinked edge the white pencil line will give you a cutting guide.

Tracing TRACING
Tinta black: dots on dice, the number on the calendar page, the edge of the spots on the toadstool cap.
Tinta sepia: the rest of the design apart from the fir needles.

Painting PAINTING
Pintura green: clover leaves.
Pintura green + a little yellow: leaves and fir needles.
Pintura red: Toadstool cap, berries.
Pintura white: Stems and dots on cap of toadstools, Calendar page.
Pintura brown + a little yellow: horseshoe.
Pintura brown: nail holes on horseshoe.

Dorsing DORSING
Dorso ochre: the area of the design.

Perforating PERFORATING
As per the perforating grid.

Embossing EMBOSSING
Toadstools, number, top edge calendar, dice, clover leaves, berries; in the perforation grid scalloped lines, dots and diagonal stripes in the whole perforation area.

CUTTING

Cutting

Cut the perforations to crosses and slots.

FINISHING OFF

Finishing off

Fold the card. You now have the choice of edges to finish off the card; either 'a' with ordinary scissors cut along traced edge or 'b' with pinking shears cut along pencilled edge or if you just want a straight edge simply cut along the white pencil line with a pair of scissors or use a craft knife.

Anniversary or general greetings card

GENERAL

General

The basket has a loose card that fits in the perforated opening amongst the flowers. Make this card on a separate piece of paper and then write on the greeting of your choice. The front page of the card is lace edged and the back page is perforated to scallops.

TRACING

Tracing

Tinta white: all the flowers.
Tinta sepia: the rest of the design.
Tinta gold: outline of the basket handle and scalloped outline on back page of card.

PAINTING

Painting

Pintura white + a very tiny bit of red: roses, and buds on handle.
Pintura purple + a little white: the two large flowers on the right.
Pintura white + a little yellow: Marguerites.
Pintura yellow + red: flower centres.
Pintura green + yellow: leaves.
Pintura blue: little flowers.
Pintura brown + yellow: basket handle and freehand thin lines between the perforations on the basket (see coloured picture for guide).
Tinta sepia: the stamens in flower centres.

DORSING

Dorsing

Dorso green: area of flowers and round the basket.
Doro ochre: basket.

1
a
b

See pages 12, 13 and 34 for patterns

Perforating PERFORATING
As per the perforation grid (also the small card on a separate piece of paper). Perforate with single needle tool along dotted line amongst the flowers.

Embossing EMBOSSING
All the flower petals, the stripes in the basket perforation grid, the handle, dots in the whole of the border perforation grid and also in the small card perforation grid.

Cutting CUTTING
Four needle combinations to crosses and slots.
Cut perforations at edge of border design on both card and small card and remove waste. Perforate back page edge along the outside of gold line scallops.

First communion

General GENERAL
The card has two folds and has the appearance of an envelope when completed. The perforation grid shown on the folded design should appear on the top right hand side of the third 'page'. Mark outlines on to parchment paper using a white pencil remembering that design is shown in folded state.

Tracing TRACING
Tinta sepia: face and hair.
Tinta gold: flower stamens, stems and beads on veil fringe.
Tinta white: the rest of the design and the scalloped front edge of card as well as the outlines round perforation grid on third 'page' and the hatching in the perforation grid.

Painting PAINTING
Pintura brown: hair
Pintura flesh (painted on reverse of card): face.

Perforating PERFORATION
As per perforation grid.

Embossing EMBOSSING
From the FRONT: the shaded area in the flowers.

See pages 16, 20 and 32 for patterns

See pages 22 and 23 for patterns

From the BACK: the rest of the flowers, the straight line and scalloped lines on front flap, dots, outline and cross hatching in perforation grid.

Cutting

CUTTING
Cut the four needle combinations to crosses and slots.

Finishing off

FINISHING OFF
Perforate the scalloped edge of front flap and the centre of the scallops out using single needle tool. Cut with scissors or perforate the wavy edge of the card as shown on pattern.

Wedding card

General

GENERAL
You have a choice of edges: if you want the straight edge then mark this with a white pencil. If you want either of the two edges shown to the side of the pattern these must be traced in white tinta to give you a cutting guide.

Tracing

TRACING
Tinta sepia: hands.
Tinta black: groom's coat sleeve and button.
Tinta white: bride's sleeve and groom's shirt cuff and scalloped front edge of card.

Painting

PAINTING
Pintura white: the wedding dress sleeve; shirt cuff.
Pintura white + a little Tinta black: coat sleeve.
Pintura flesh (painted on the reverse of the card): hands.
Pintura white with red: the bride's nails.
Tinta gold: rings.

Perforating

PERFORATION
As per perforation grid.

Embossing

EMBOSSING
Bride's sleeve, design in perforation grid, scalloped edge front card, rings, groom's shirt cuff and very lightly groom's sleeve.

Cutting CUTTING
Cut the perforations to crosses.

Finishing off FINISHING OFF
Front page: perforate along the scalloped edge.
Fold the card and finish edge of choice using scissors or a craft knife.

Mother's day card

Tracing TRACING
Tinta sepia: leaves and veins in leaves; stems.
Tinta red: rose petals and buds.
Tinta gold: card edges.

Painting PAINTING
Pintura green + a little yellow: leaves and stems.
Pintura white + a little red: rose petals and rose bud.

Dorsing DORSING
Dorso green: area of flower design.

Perforating PERFORATING
As per perforation grid.

Embossing EMBOSSING
Rose, rose bud, design in perforation grid, border lines of card (N.B. the card in the photograph is finished off and embossed differently).

Cutting CUTTING
Perforations to crosses and slots. Perforate round front edge and cut back edge straight. Alternatively you can perforate through both layers of card making the back and front edge the same.

Get well soon

Tracing TRACING
Tinta sepia: whole of design

Painting PAINTING
Pintura white: nurses hat and shoes.
Pintura yellow: bandage and rolls of bandages.
Pintura red: cross on nurses hat, mouth and cat's mouth.
Pintura blue + a little black: dress.
Pintura white + a little tinta black: cat, ribbon and scissors.
Tinta black: soles of shoes, eyelashes (also on cat).
Pintura brown + a little yellow: hair, stool.
Pintura flesh (painted on the back): face and hands.

Dorsing DORSING
Dorso green: ground.

Perforating PERFORATING.
As per perforation grid.

Embossing EMBOSSING
Ribbon, shoes, head and paws of cat, sleeves, hair (stripes), bandages, legs of stool, scissors, design and wavy lines in perforation grid.

Cutting CUTTING
Cut perforations to crosses and slots.

Finishing off FINISHING OFF
Fold card and perforate round scalloped edge going through both layers of paper.

Birth of a baby

Tracing TRACING
Tinta gold: egg.
Tinta sepia: rest of design.

Painting PAINTING
Pintura white + a little blue: nappy.
Pintura blue: eyes (black dot for pupil).
Pintura flesh + a little white: outside of egg shell.
Pintura white: inside of egg shell.
Pintura yellow: hair (also paint in fine strips of brown).
Pintura green: leaves, stems and clumps of grass.

See pages 29 and 35 for patterns

See pages 24 and 32 for patterns

Pintura white + a little red: flowers.
Pintura flesh (on the reverse of card): baby.
Tinta gold: lines in perforation grid.

DORSING

Dorsing

Dorso green: grass area.
Dorso blue: sky area.

PERFORATING

Perforating

As per the perforation grid.

EMBOSSING

Embossing

The beige sections of the egg shell, nappy, flowers, thick lines and dots in perforation grid.

CUTTING

Cutting

Cut the perforations to crosses and slots.
Fold card and perforate round the edge going through both layers.

Christmas card

GENERAL

General

There are five 3-D elements in the pattern which must be traced onto a spare piece of paper, coloured, embossed and perforated out then stuck on with Pergakit.

TRACING

Tracing

Tinta gold: flame, candle, edge of candle grease, baubles, flower.
Tinta red: berries.
Tinta sepia: holly leaves and flower stamens.

PAINTING

Painting

Pintura yellow: flame, candle, flower centre.
Pintura brown + yellow: fine lines in flame.
Pintura green + little yellow: holly leaves and fir needles.
Pintura white + red: large flower and bud.
Pintura red: berries.
Pintura blue: on the baubles, purple and fuchsia for the other two baubles and red for the small bauble.

Dorsing DORSING
Dorso ochre: area round flame.

Perforating PERFORATING
As per perforation grid.

Embossing EMBOSSING
Flame, candle grease, flower petals, berries, baubles, dark areas in back page border pattern; dots and wavy lines in perforation grid.

Cutting CUTTING
Perforations to crosses and slots.

Finishing off FINISHING OFF
Perforate round card edge (and perforating out the middle of scallops as per photo).
Affix the 3-D elements to card with Pergakit.
Glitter can be added to candle grease and baubles by painting them with clear nail varnish and scattering the glitter on whilst wet.

5.2 MISCELLANEOUS

Gift tags

General GENERAL
Make the gift tags to suit your own taste. If you want some guidance then these are the instructions for the patterns shown on page 36.
Top left: flowers: red, ribbon: blue, leaves: green. Emboss ribbon and flowers.
Top right: flowers: purple and red, leaves: green, hearts: red. Emboss hearts and flowers.
Bottom middle: Trace the butterfly on a spare piece of parchment and perforate out butterfly and wavy border: gold. Emboss the pattern in the perforation grid and parts of butterfly. Perforate out the pieces of the butterfly wings as indicated. Attach the butterfly to a corner of the gift tag with Pergakit.

Patterns on page 37

Top left: nappy blue with white dots, label yellow, baby flesh, hair yellow. Emboss nappy, label, hair and wavy line.

Top right: scalloped line gold, perforate as per grid, emboss and cut to slots.

Bottom middle: perforate as per grid, emboss dots in grid, cut to crosses, with single needle pierce a hole in the middle of each embossed dot, cut outside edge of perforation grid and remove waste paper.

Envelope card

GENERAL

General

This is a two fold card with 3-D flowers on flap.

TRACING

Tracing

Tinta blue: line round perforation grid, 10 3-D flowers and strips in the petals.
Tinta white: outline.

DORSING

Dorsing

Dorso blue: whole of card except the flap front.

PERFORATE

Perforating

As per perforation grid.

EMBOSSING

Embossing

From the FRONT: the petals of the 3-D elements.
From the BACK: the design and dark lines on the whole of the perforation grid. The outside edge of flap.

CUTTING

Cutting

Perforations to crosses and slots.

FINISHING OFF

Finishing off

Fold the paper to envelope (the sides remain open). Perforate out the ten flowers and attach these with Pergakit to the areas marked with an ‘x’ on pattern.
Cut the straight sides of the card with pinking shears and emboss a line between the teeth as per pattern.

Flower heart

Tracing

TRACING
Tinta sepia: on the front page the whole of the design;
Tinta white: on the back page scalloped and 'v' lines of border.

Painting

PAINTING
Paint the pansies in the following colours:
Pintura violet and yellow: 4 flowers.
Pintura violet: 4 flowers.
Pintura red: 4 flowers.
Pintura fuchsia: 4 flowers.
Pintura violet + a little white: ribbon.
Pintura green: leaves.
Tinta green + sepia: stripes on pansy petals.
Pintura yellow: flower centres.
Tinta sepia: dots for stamens.

Perforating

PERFORATING
As per perforation grid.

Embossing

EMBOSSING
All the flower petals, ribbon and the design in the whole of the perforation grid on front page and the 'v' forms on back page as per illustration on page 15.

Cutting

CUTTING
Perforations to crosses and slots.

Finishing off

FINISHING OFF
Front page: cut through the outer edge of the perforations and remove waste paper.
Back page: cut straight.

Brooches and a doily

Brooches are easy and quick to make. The following are general instructions.
Frames: brooches with loose backs and glass: 5cm round or 5 x 2.5cm oval.

Tracing: Tinta white and/or gold.
Dorsing: to taste.
Embossing: thick and thin lines and dots.
Perforating: as per grids.
Cutting: to crosses etc.
Finishing off: mount pattern in brooch blank.

Doily

As you can see from the photograph a coloured piece of paper has been attached behind the finished design. N.B. the design in the photograph is different from the pattern given.

Winter landscape

General

GENERAL
This design has four 3-D elements marked with an 'x' on the pattern (3 roof pieces and flower top left). Use a piece of scrap parchment paper to trace these and then perforate out and affix to design with Pergakit.

Tracing

TRACING
Tinta sepia: house, fence posts, stamens, tree trunks, stars, leaves, veins in leaves and line of horizon.
Tinta red: flowers, berries and ribbon.
Tinta white: roofs.

Painting

PAINTING
Pintura red + little white: ribbon, flowers.
Pintura red: berries.
Pintura green + little yellow: flower centres, leaves.
Pintura brown: tree trunks, fence posts, doors and windows.
Pintura white: snow on tree and fence posts; eaves of porch and large roof; 3-D roofs, highlight on berries.
Pintura green: clumps of grass.

Dorsing

DORSING
Dorso green: the grass area both sides of the path.
Dorso ochre: sky.

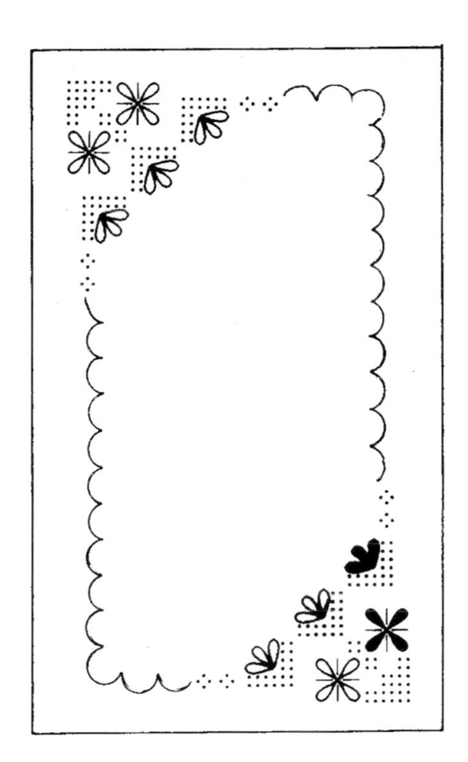

See pages 32 and 34 for patterns

See page 44 for pattern

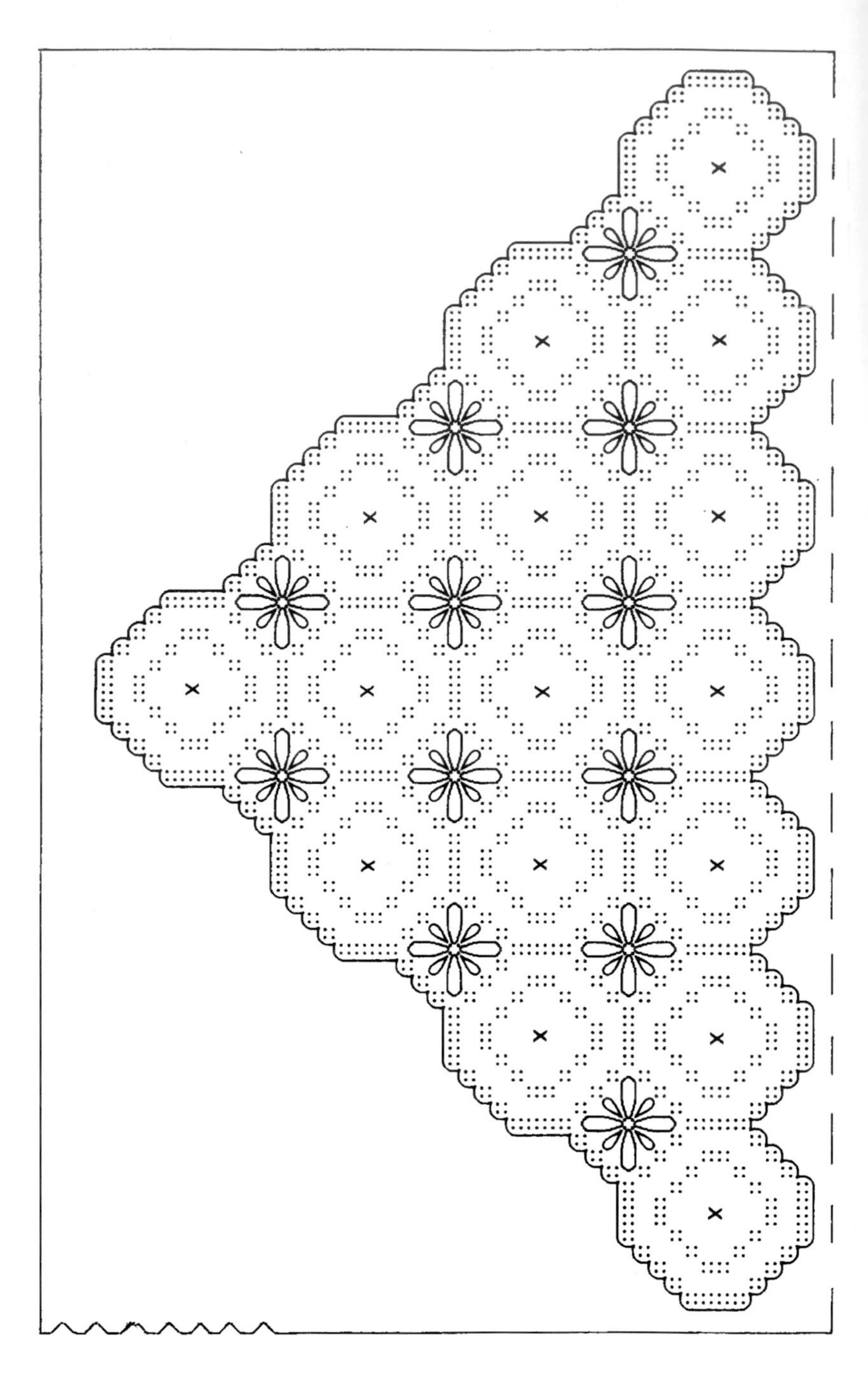

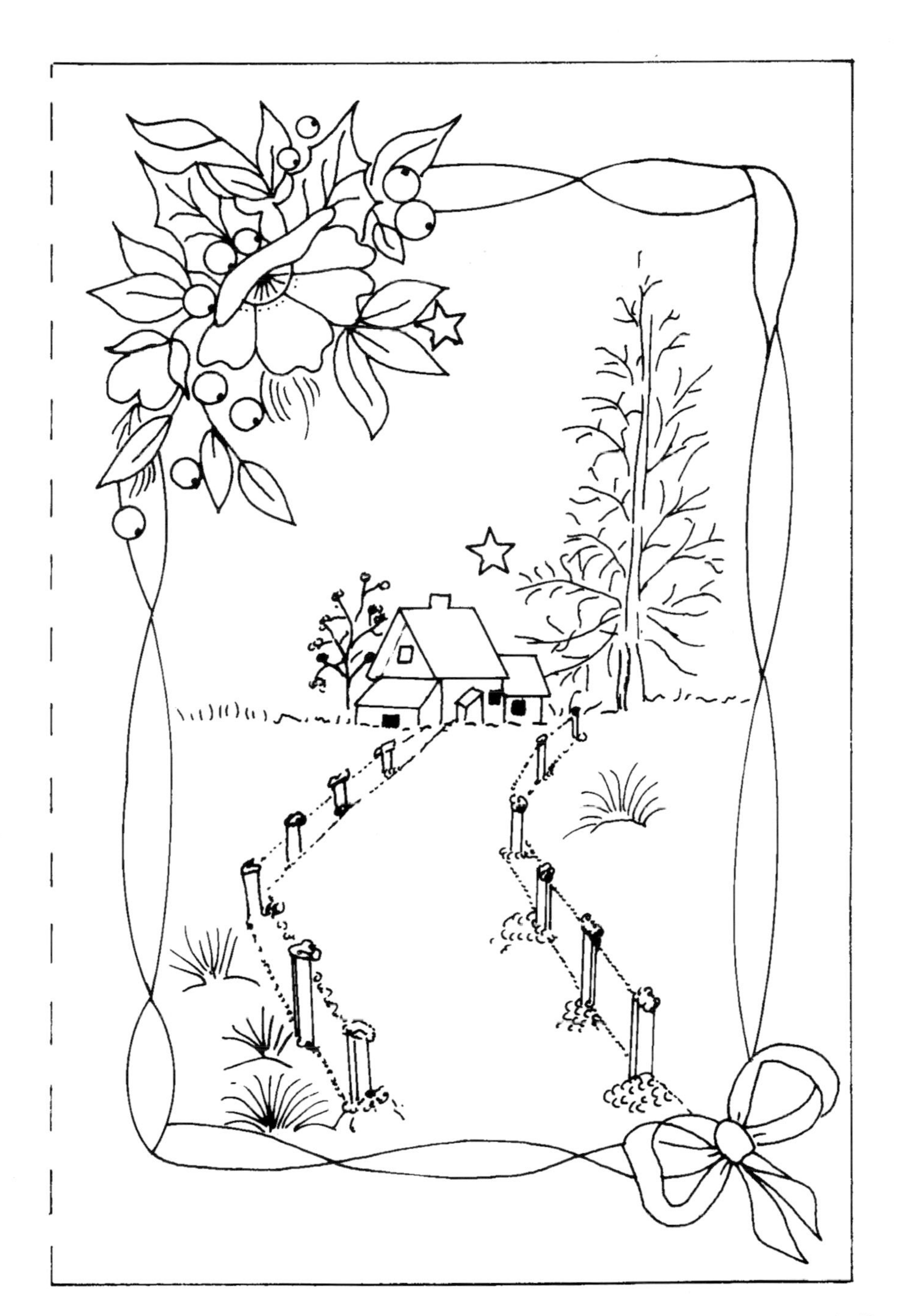

Finishing off

EMBOSSING
Berries, stars, tree trunk, flowers, fence posts, roofs and ribbon.

FINISHING OFF
Perforate or cut out the 3-D elements and affix to card with Pergakit. When affixing flower and largest roof in place make sure that you leave a 3mm clearance between element and card.
Small roofs leave 1mm clearance.
Cut the edges of the card either straight or to choice.

General

Tracing

Fantasy flower design

GENERAL
You have several choices of card finishing. The fold line can be at the top or to the left: you can fold card and cut the edges to the outer edges shown or you can perforate round the outside edge of the flower design as seen in the photograph on page 39. Be careful not to go through the fold.

Painting

TRACING
Tinta white: whole design.

Perforating

PAINTING
Tinta gold: all the stems (shown by dark lines on design).

Embossing

DORSING
Dorso green: the whole of the back page.
Dorso the flowers as per the photograph.

Cutting

EMBOSSING
The areas marked with a ‘c’; the cross hatching on leaves and petals as per the photograph are done with the single needle tool. If cutting card straight: emboss between the double lines round edges of design.

Finishing off

PERFORATING
As per the grid and then cut to crosses and slots: perforate out all the pieces between the stems (for guidance some have been marked with an ‘x’).
FINISHING OFF

C
X
C
X
X
X
X
X
C
C

Either perforate round outer edge or cut edges straight depending on which finish you have chosen.

Fantasy picture

GENERAL
Picture frame: 25 x 20 cm.
Mount: 25 x 20 cm matt black mounting board.
Parchment paper: cut finished piece to 20 x 14.5 cm.
3-D elements: there are four flowers.

TRACING
Tinta white: butterfly wings.
Tinta sepia: butterfly body (fill in outlines), feelers, flowers and also the 3-D flower elements.
Tinta gold: the thick lines round the outer edges of the perforation grids.

PAINTING
Pintura yellow: flower centres.
Tinta black: stamens.

PERFORATING
As per perforation grid.

EMBOSSING
Stripes and dots in the whole of the perforation grids, butterfly body, thick gold lines round grids.
On the FRONT: flower petals on 3-D elements.

CUTTING
Cut perforations to crosses and slots, perforate out the pieces of the pattern marked with a cross. Perforate out the 3-D elements.

FINISHING OFF
With Pergakit affix the 3-D flowers in place placing them so that the flower petals on the actual design show (see photo). Scatter glitter on the inner rings of the butterfly wings and also on the flowers (use clear nail varnish then scatter the glitter). Mount in the frame with or without glass.

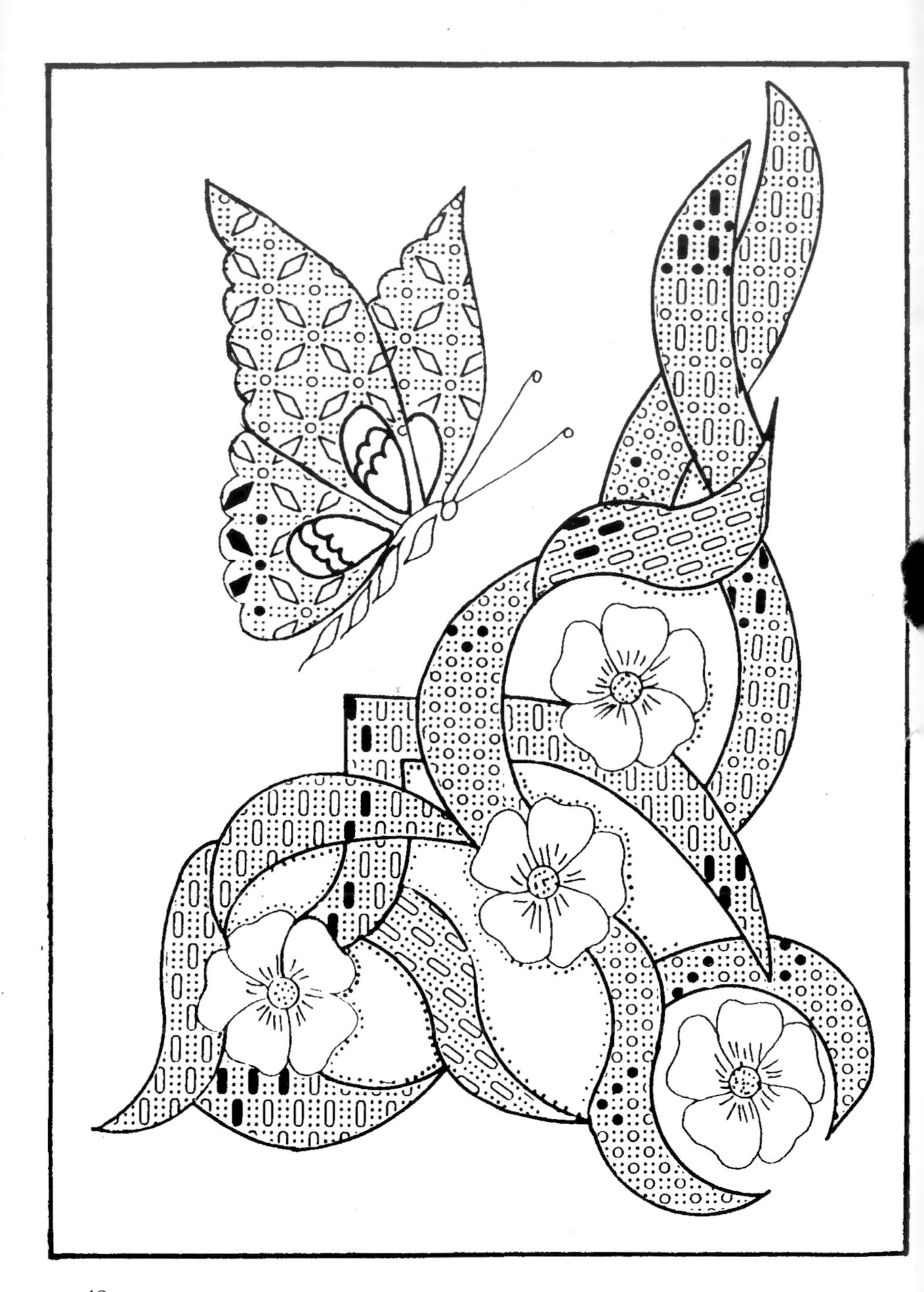